The San Francisco Earthquake of 1906: The Story of the Deadliest Earthquake in American History

By Charles River Editors

Arnold Genthe's photo of Sacramento St. with fire off in the distance

D0752543

About Charles River Editors

Charles River Editors provides superior editing and original writing services across the digital publishing industry, with the expertise to create digital content for publishers across a vast range of subject matter. In addition to providing original digital content for third party publishers, we also republish civilization's greatest literary works, bringing them to new generations of readers via ebooks.

Sign up here to receive updates about free books as we publish them, and visit Our Kindle Author Page to browse today's free promotions and our most recently published Kindle titles.

Introduction

Picture of the ruins after the earthquake and fires

The San Francisco Earthquake of 1906

"[I]t does not seem to have affected any one with a sense of final destruction, with any foreboding of irreparable disaster. Every one is talking of it this afternoon, and no one is in the least degree dismayed. I have talked and listened in two clubs, watched people in cars and in the street, and one man is glad that Chinatown will be cleared out for good; another's chief solicitude is for Millet's 'Man with the Hoe.' 'They'll cut it out of the frame,' he says, a little anxiously. 'Sure.' But there is no doubt anywhere that San Francisco can be rebuilt, larger, better, and soon. Just as there would be none at all if all this New York that has so obsessed me with its limitless bigness was itself a blazing ruin. I believe these people would more than half like the situation." – H.G. Wells

On April 18, 1906, most of the residents of the city of San Francisco were sound asleep when the ground started to shake around 5:15 a.m., but what started as fairly soft tremors turned into a violent shaking in all directions. The roar of the earthquake unquestionably woke up residents, at least those fortunate enough not to be immediately swallowed by the cracks opening up in the ground. The earthquake lasted about a minute, but it had enough destructive force to divert the course of entire rivers and level much of the 9th largest city in America at the time.

Unfortunately for San Franciscans, the worst was yet to come. During the earthquake, the city's gas mains and water mains were ruptured, which had the effects of starting a number of fires and preventing the residents from being equipped to fight them. Without water to truly fight the blaze, the city's officials actually resorted to demolishing buildings in hopes of containing the fire, and witnesses reported seeing San Franciscans trapped in the burning buildings being shot by authorities instead of letting them burn alive. The fires lasted three days, and by the time they were done, 80% of the city was in ruins, about 60% of the residents were homeless, and an estimated 3,000-6,000 were dead. In fact, the fires were so devastating that contemporary San Franciscans called the disaster "The Fire."

Although the resulting fires may have done the most damage, the widespread destruction made clear to city leaders that the new buildings would need better safety codes and protection against subsequent earthquakes. The city reinforced new buildings against earthquakes and fixed older surviving buildings to better deal with future earthquakes, and the city also created the Auxiliary Water Supply System to prevent a repeat of the 1906 disaster.

At the same time, there was a determined sense of resolve to rebuild San Francisco into a bigger and better city, and financial assistance flowed to the shattered city from all across the country. Even as refugee camps were set up in parks and sheltered people for a few years, the U.S. Army and other volunteers helped provide for the people, and despite suffering damage amounting to the equivalent of over $6 billion in today's dollars, California governor George C. Pardee was right when he predicted, "This is not the first time that San Francisco has been destroyed by fire, I have not the slightest doubt that the City by the Golden Gate will be speedily rebuilt, and will, almost before we know it, resume her former great activity."

The San Francisco Earthquake of 1906: The Deadliest Earthquake in American History chronicles the deadliest natural disaster in California's history and one of the most important seismic events on record. Along with pictures of important people, places, and events, you will learn about the San Francisco Earthquake of 1906 like never before, in no time at all.

The San Francisco Earthquake of 1906: The Story of the Deadliest Earthquake in American History

About Charles River Editors

Introduction

Chapter 1: San Francisco Before the Quake

"Jesus left the temple and was walking away when his disciples came up to him to call his attention to its buildings. 'Do you see all these things?' he asked. 'Truly I tell you, not one stone here will be left on another; everyone will be thrown down…There will be famines and earthquakes in various places…For in the days before the flood, people were eating and drinking, marrying and giving in marriage, up to the day Noah entered the ark; and they knew nothing about what would happen until the flood came and took them all away." - Matthew 24:1-2

Whenever a natural disaster strikes, people often assume that there was no way to see it coming, but while that is sometimes the case, there is usually evidence that something bad is about to happen. Such was the case with the earthquake that struck San Francisco on April 18, 1906. Nearly six weeks before it struck, Professor Alexander McAdie recorded a small earthquake in San Francisco, and such small quakes were sometimes precursors to larger problems. However, McAdie also realized that small earthquakes could often be one-time events that didn't signify anything else coming, and San Francisco's location near the San Andreas fault line ensured the city was used to small rumblings. In essence, if McAdie correctly predicted that a bigger earthquake was coming, he would be a hero, but if not, he would find himself a laughingstock. That left him in a conundrum.

Meanwhile, San Francisco had other problems on its mind. It had been a relatively small town until the California gold rush just 60 years earlier, but with people heading west hoping to strike it rich, the city had grown by leaps and bounds. Its population continued swelling with more men looking for gold, more women coming with their husbands, and more businesses looking for customers. Unlike more settled parts of the country that had grown up slowly around entrenched families, San Francisco was a boom town, but at about 60 years old, it had also begun to show its age. Those in charge had their hands full trying to keep the city healthy and looking good, which required a constant influx of services and workers, but by 1906, conflicts between the two had led to unionization and labor unrest. On April 17, the day before the earthquake, Waiters Union threatened to go out on strike.

Then there was the issue of the railroads. San Francisco depended on America's iron arteries to bring in supplies and ship out goods, but railroad companies were also well aware of their importance and happily used it to get what they wanted, including the use of streetcars above ground instead of an underground subway. As the city's leaders considered the proposals before them, more rumors swarmed about bribes and threats being used to buy influence. San Francisco's mayor, "Handsome Gene" Schmitz, was popular among the union leaders and in 1901 became the first member of the recently-formed Union Labor Party to be elected mayor of an American city. However, in 1906, he found himself under scrutiny and accused by many of graft and taking bribes, and not long after the disaster, he would be indicted and convicted on 27 counts of political corruption. His conviction would later be overturned before he served any jail time.

Schmitz

Problems with the railroad were soon overshadowed by issues related to the city's water supply. The day before the earthquake struck, Mayor Schmitz was mulling what to do about the city's plans to divert the nearby Toulumne River so that its water could be used by the citizens of the city. Water in California had always been an issue, especially since the state was quickly becoming more populated that her supplies could support. Of course, there were competing interests for the water, and the President of the nearby Modesto Irrigation District was displeased about the prospect of losing some of his own share of the river that he wrote a complaint to the mayor that was received on April 17.

As the sun went down on April 17, most San Franciscans retired to their homes or to the opera house, where the famous Italian tenor Enrico Caruso was performing. The city fathers were proud to host such a famous singer and looked at it as evidence that their town was growing up and developing a level of culture that might someday rival the cities back east. Caruso himself was pleased with his performance and his reception, later writing, "I was stopping at the [Palace] Hotel, where many of my fellow-artists were staying, and very comfortable it was. I had a room on the fifth floor, and on Tuesday evening, the night before the great catastrophe, I went to bed feeling very contented. I had sung in "Carmen" that night, and the opera had one with fine éclat. We were all pleased, and, as I said before, I went to bed that night feeling happy and contented."

An illustration of the Palace Hotel (which was destroyed during the disaster)

Others were literally "marrying and giving in marriage." Dr. George Blumer later wrote, "On the evening of April 17th 1906…I acted as best man at the wedding of my old friend Doctor August Jerome Lartigan to Doctor Kate Brady. It was a church wedding and was followed by a beautiful supper at the home of the bride's parents out in the Mission. I did not get to bed until about 1:30 a.m. on the morning of April 18th."

Many people, especially those living near the warehouse district, were awakened suddenly by sirens wailing, but it wasn't due to the earthquake. Instead, it was a three alarm fire at the Central California Canneries located at the corner of Bay and Mason Streets. The fire broke out sometime before 11:00 p.m. and was already in fully fury when the fire department was called. By the time the last flame was doused and the firemen were able to return to their houses, it was nearly 5:00 in the morning. Barely taking time to strip off their soot-stained clothes and wash their faces, they collapsed into their beds and fell quickly into a sound sleep. The ensuing 20 minute nap was the last real rest any of them would get for days.

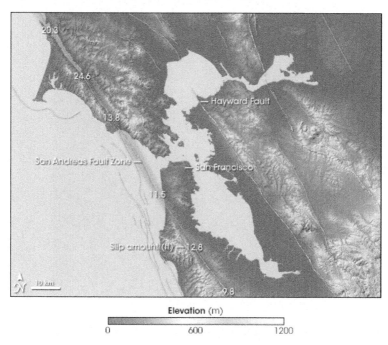

The San Andreas fault zone and its proximity to San Francisco

Caruso

Chapter 2: The Earthquake

"I had $600.00 in gold under my pillow. I awoke as I was thrown out of bed. Attempting to walk, the floor shook so that I fell. I grabbed my clothing and rushed down into the office, where dozens were already congregated. Suddenly the lights went out, and every one rushed for the door. Outside I witnessed a sight I never want to see again. It was dawn and light. I looked up. The air was filled with falling stones. People around me were crushed to death on all sides. All around the huge buildings were shaking and waving. Every moment there were reports like 100 cannons going off at one time. Then streams of fire would shoot out, and other reports followed. I asked a man standing next to me what happened. Before he could answer a thousand bricks fell on him and he was killed. A woman threw her arms around my neck. I pushed her away and fled. All around me buildings were rocking and flames shooting. As I ran people on all sides were crying, praying and calling for help. I thought the end of the world had come." – G.A. Raymond

For most people, the San Francisco Earthquake of 1906 came as a rude awakening, literally. When the quake began on April 18 at 5:15 in the morning, most people were still sound asleep in their beds. Arnold Genthe had been at the opera house the night before and recalled, "After a quiet supper party with some friends, I walked home and went to bed with the music of Carmen still singing in my ears. It seemed as if I had scarcely been asleep when I was awakened by a terrifying sound–the Chinese porcelains that I had been collecting in the last years had crashed to the floor…The whole house was creaking and shaking, the chandelier was swinging like a pendulum, and I felt as if I were on a ship tossed about by a rough sea. 'This can't go on much longer,' I said to myself. 'When a house shakes like this, the ceiling is bound to collapse. As soon as the plaster begins to fall, I'll cover my head and accept what comes.'"

Peter Bacigalupi had a similar experience: "On the morning of the 18th of April I was awakened from a sound slumber by a terrific trembling, which acted in the same manner as would a bucking bronco. I sat up in bed with a start. My bed was going up and down in all four directions at once, while all about me I heard screams, wails, and crashing of breaking china-ware and nick-nacks. I was very quietly watching the clock on the mantel, which was doing a fancy stunt, while the ornaments in the parlor could be heard crashing to the floor. A great portion of plaster right over the head of my bed fell all around me, and caused a cloud of dust, which was very hard to breathe through."

A toppled statue 30 miles away from San Francisco on the Stanford University campus

Of course, not everyone was asleep. Thomas Chase was on his way to work and thus had the unique experience of seeing the effects of the earthquake in action on the streets: "I heard a low distant rumble. It was coming from the west. Louder and louder. I stopped and listened. Then it hit. Power and trolley lines snapped like threads. The ends of the power lines dropped to the pavement not 10 feet from where I stood, writhing and hissing like reptiles. Brick and glass showered about me. Buildings along First Street from Howard to Market crumbled like card houses. One was brick. Not a soul escaped. Clouds of that obliterated the scene of destruction. The dust hung low over the rubble in the street."

Picture of the damage on Howard St.

The SS *Columbia* lying up against a dry dock

Another eyewitness who was already awake at the time described similar experiences: "Of a sudden we had found ourselves staggering and reeling. It was as if the earth was slipping gently from under our feet. Then came the sickening swaying of the earth that threw us flat upon our faces. We struggled in the street. We could not get on our feet. Then it seemed as though my head were split with the roar that crashed into my ears. Big buildings were crumbling as one might crush a biscuit in one's hand. Ahead of me a great cornice crushed a man as if he were a maggot - a laborer in overalls on his way to the Union Iron Works with a dinner pail on his arm."

One of the men on the streets, G.A. Raymond, explained how he escaped to safety on Market St.: "I met a Catholic priest, and he said: 'We must get to the ferry.' He knew the way, and we rushed down Market Street. Men, women and children were crawling from the debris. Hundreds were rushing down the street and every minute people were felled by debris. At places the streets had cracked and opened. Chasms extended in all directions. I saw a drove of cattle, wild with fright, rushing up Market Street. I crouched beside a swaying building. As they came nearer they disappeared, seeming to drop out into the earth. When the last had gone I went nearer and found they had indeed been precipitated into the earth, a wide fissure having swallowed them. I was crazy with fear and the horrible sights. How I reached the ferry I cannot say. It was bedlam, pandemonium and hell rolled into one. There must have been 10,000 people trying to get on that boat. Men and women fought like wildcats to push their way aboard. Clothes were torn from the backs of men and women and children indiscriminately. Women fainted, and there was no water at hand with which to revive them. Men lost their reason at those awful moments. One big, strong man, beat his head against one of the iron pillars on the dock, and cried out in a loud voice: 'This fire must be put out! The city must be saved!' It was awful."

Among the more than 1,000 people who lost their lives that day, hundreds died instantly when their homes collapsed around them. For instance, many of the poorest citizens of the city lived in the South-of-Market tenements, and those poorly made apartments collapsed under their feet before they even had time to get out of bed or understand what was happening. Some of them were likely lucky enough to die instantly, but many remained injured and trapped for hours before passing away. The most fortunate residents managed to dig their way out of the rubble, often with the help of firemen or the neighbors.

As with many similar disasters, many of those who were killed were firefighters, and the first one injured was not trying to save others. In fact, Fire Chief Engineer Dennis T. Sullivan was asleep in the fire house when he suffered a mortal injury. In a terse, official report, Battalion Chief Walter Cook described what happened: "On the 18th inst. at 5:13 a.m. our quarters were carried down by the dome of the California Hotel...The roof and third and second floor came down through the apparatus floor to the cellar. Apparatus floor resting on coal pile; Third floor occupied by the late Chief and his wife...When the crash ceased we started at once to dig for the Chief and Mrs. Sullivan.... While so digging the Chief walked from the rear of the pile. P. Gallagher and Jerry Collins, Chief's Operator, assisted him into the St. George Stables. Chief's Operator, drove him away at once to the Hospital. Mrs. Sullivan was taken out shortly afterwards and we carried her into the California Hotel where a Doctor took charge of her." At first, it seemed that Sullivan was not seriously injured, but he had been badly burned when he landed next to a broken radiator and died a few days later. Upon Sullivan's death, John Dougherty suddenly became the Acting Chief, just in time for the biggest crisis to ever hit the city.

Another fireman, James O'Neill, was also killed before he ever got to fight the famous blaze. He was watering the horses outside his station when the quake hit, and when the American Hotel collapsed next door, one of the walls fell onto the fire station and O'Neill himself. Officer Max

Fenner, a cop walking his beat, was also killed by a falling wall that morning. According to Police Captain Thomas Duke, Fenner "was standing opposite the Essex Lodging House, a seven-story brick building on Mason near Ellis Street, when the earthquake occurred. He observed that the front wall of the building was tottering and at the same time he saw a woman run out of the building onto the sidewalk. He tried to warn her of her danger, but as she did not move he rushed over toward her. Just then the whole front of the building fell out, and while the woman ran inside the doorway and was unharmed, Fenner was instantly killed…" Looking back, it soon became obvious that the only reason more people weren't killed by buildings collapsing into the streets was that it was so early in the morning.

A picture of Stockton St. from Union Square

Though most of the damage was centered in and around San Francisco, the quake itself was felt as far away as Los Angeles. Author Jack London felt it on his ranch in Glen Ellen and wrote to a family member, "Routed out of bed at a quarter past five. Half an hour later Mrs. London and I were in the saddle. We rode miles over the surrounding country. An hour after the shock, from a high place in the mountains, we could see at the same time the smoke of burning San Francisco and of burning Santa Rosa. Caught a train to Santa Rosa – Santa Rosa got it worse than S.F. Then in the afternoon, Wednesday afternoon, we got into San Francisco and spent the whole night in the path of the flames – you bet, I saw it all."

City Hall in ruins after the earthquake

Chapter 3: Help

"I was living with my family at 1310 Washington Street, near Jones, one of the most elevated parts of the city, and was awakened by the earthquake shock at 5:16 a.m…The entire street-car system being brought to a standstill by the damage resulting from the shock, I hastened on foot toward the business section of the city for the purpose of ascertaining what damage had been done to the hotels and other large buildings…I realized then that a great conflagration was inevitable, and that the city police force would not be able to maintain the fire-lines and protect public and private property over the great area affected. It was at once determined to order out all available troops not only for the purpose of guarding federal buildings, but to aid the police- and fire-departments of the city." - General Frederick Funston

Within minutes of the quake subsiding, General Frederick Funston, commander of nearby Fort Mason, knew that he and other leaders of the city were facing a catastrophe of epic proportions. He immediately dispatched a note to the fort ordering all available men to report for duty at the Hall of Justice and to put themselves as the disposal of Mayor Schmitz. His decisive thinking no doubt saved numerous lives and thousands of dollars in property, as it provided the city leaders with resources to get on top of the looting situation right away.

Funston

The troops arrived at around 7:00 a.m. and were quickly dispatched to patrol different parts of the city, and when a serious aftershock occurred at 8:14, they were on hand to help calm the public and manage the crowds milling about in panic. They would stay quite busy with crowd control as more than 130 more aftershocks shook the ground before the day was over. More soldiers arrived by boat from the headquarters of the First Battalion 22nd Infantry at around 10:00. A few minutes later, Admiral Casper Goodrich of the USS *Chicago* received a telegram informing him of the earthquake, and he quickly ordered his men to prepare to make way at full speed for the city. Only later would historians realized that this marked the first time the telegraph was used during a natural disaster.

The USS *Preble*, stationed out of Mare Island, was also on its way by this time and sent ashore a party of doctors and other medical personnel at around 10:30. After landing near the end of Howard Street, they acted as emergency treatment teams, caring for those injured until they could be taken to the Harbor Emergency Hospital. Their help was certainly needed, as Dr.

Blumer later recalled: "The third day I volunteered for work at the Harbor Emergency Hospital, the only undamaged one. This was because the Embarcadero between the city and the waterfront was so wide that the fire did not reach structures on the bay. During the 48 hours after the quake this hospital had a patient every two minutes. I recall seeing one patient with smallpox who was temporarily isolated out on a wharf, one sailor with a gunshot wound received while preventing looting, and a good many drug habitués, mostly courtesans from the Barbary Coast district, who could not get their morphine from the usual sources and would come to the hospital and beg for it."

What the soldiers saw when they arrived in the city was shocking even for the most battle hardened among them. What just a few hours earlier had been a thriving cultural and financial center now lay in ruins, the sounds of piano music and horse hooves having been replaced by an eerie silence punctuated by the moans of the injured and the screams of survivors searching for missing loved ones. In a world 40 years removed from large scale bombing attacks, no man there had ever seen anything like it. The commander of the *Chicago* later reported, "The city on the Fort Mason side of the harbor was, at this time, in full blaze. The buildings within the limits of the post were in danger. The air was filled with burning cinders which were blown by the wind far into the harbor and all the awnings on board had to be furled and the decks wet down to prevent fire. Thousands of panic stricken, homeless and destitute people thronged the shore in the neighborhood of the Fort. Food was being supplied but there had not yet been time for any well-organized system of distribution. Drinking water was difficult to find. All were eager to leave but no transportation was immediately available."

No one had time to stand around and take in the full magnitude of what they were seeing because fires were already breaking out around them, and there were still living people who could be rescued if they acted quickly. Most of all, there were throngs of panicked people determined to flee to the hills who had be managed. Bacigalupi ran into these crowds as he tried to make his way to his record store and described the chaos: "I hurried as much as possible, but did not make much headway owing to the fact that the majority of people were hurrying in the opposite direction to which I was going. They were taking to the hills. Some were dragging trunks; others carrying valises on their shoulders. I saw more talking machines in that one day than I believe I will ever see all together again in one time. It seems that the first thought of the owners of these machines was to save them in preference to anything else. There were also a great many comical sights such as a woman carrying ironing boards and an iron. One woman carried a parrot's cage in one hand, while in the other was a bundle of clothes, hurriedly gathered together. I noticed that the bottom of the cage was gone, having doubtlessly dropped out on the way without being missed."

A picture of residents along Market St. taken from the Ferry Building Tower

A picture of people trying to get out of the city

Chapter 4: Fire

Picture of the fire spreading near the Mission District

"On Wednesday morning at a quarter past five came the earthquake. A minute later the flames were leaping upward In a dozen different quarters south of Market Street, in the working-class ghetto, and in the factories, fires started. There was no opposing the flames. There was no organization, no communication. All the cunning adjustments of a twentieth century city had been smashed by the earthquake. The streets were humped into ridges and depressions, and piled with the debris of fallen walls. The steel rails were twisted into perpendicular and horizontal angles. The telephone and telegraph systems were disrupted. And the great water-mains had burst. All the shrewd contrivances and safeguards of man had been thrown out of gear by thirty seconds' twitching of the earth-crust." - Jack London

As destructive and deadly as the earthquake was, the worst destruction came not because of the buildings that fell but because of those that burned. Within moments of the tremors fading away, fires began to break out all over the city, caused and fed primarily by a combination of broken gas lines and open flames. Had other factors not aligned to allow their spread, the destruction still might have been held to a minimum, but the earthquake brought about the city's eventual decimation by limiting the method by which firemen could be dispatched. In his report, Fire Alarm Operator James Kelly explained, "Within a very few seconds after the shock ended I saw the smoke of an apparently large fire begin to rise from what I judged to be the vicinity of Market and Beale St. I at once went to key to strike out said box. No alarm came in for this fire, and be it noted that no alarms whatsoever came into the office after the commencement of the earthquake. Attempting to tap out as said, I at once found striker battery open. I rushed to battery room, saw battery jar broken; disconnected it and closed circuit; rushed back to key, found that I then had current on striker battery, but found the lines all open, and that I could not send signal out. Went then at once to the Tangent Galvanometer and tested out all of my lines, and found them all open."

To understand the magnitude of what Kelly wrote, it is important to note that a line was "open" if it was broken and not working. Furthermore, before he could attempt to trigger any other fire alarms, Kelly found himself battling a blaze in his own office: "The shock broke the chimney containing this fire place, and threw the fire out into the office. About the time I found my lines gone I tried to draw water from the faucets in the office to put out this fire, but found water gone. Water however flooded into the operating room in large quantities, and with this the fires were extinguished in the office." One can only imagine his angst as he watched the city he was charged with protecting go up in flames: "Within the next few minutes after noting the fire at Market and Beale Sts. as said, I counted five additional fires starting, at different points in view from the front windows of the office. One seemingly at California and Battery Sts.; one about Sacramento and Battery; another about Bush and Market, and the others in places which I did not so closely locate. About fifteen minutes after shock ceased, Battalion Chief McClusky called me up over a Police Box 'Phone, and asked me to send engines to Gas Works, as they had blown up. I told him of conditions, and that I could count some six fires toward the water front, and, giving him the general location of said fires, suggested that he get engines down to them if he could. He said all right, and within a short time I saw an engine coming, cutting its way through fallen wires and debris."

Kelly's reference to the debris in the roads explains the third cause of the fire damage, the fact that firefighters were unable to get to the blazes in a timely manner because broken walls and buildings were blocking the streets. Also, those streets that were not blocked by debris were often made just as impassable by the crowds of people fleeing the city. But ultimately, it was the lack of water to fight the fires that proved the most damning, because the same tremors that had broken the gas lines had also broken the waters lines. Again and again, firefighters would arrive at an area only to learn that the only water they had for battling the blaze was what they carried in their own tanks, and even that was soon drained.

That is not to say that there was no water at all to be had anywhere, especially early on. In his report, a fireman with the last name of Shaughnessy wrote, "At the fire which destroyed the building at the northwest corner of Mission and 22nd streets immediately after the earthquake, there was no water to be had east of Valencia Street, but the double hydrant at the northwest corner of 22nd and Valencia and the southwest corner of Valencia and 21st St. furnished an abundant supply, which, with the aid of the cistern at 22nd and Shotwell St., extinguished the fire. At the fire at the northwest corner of Hayes and Laguna streets, almost immediately after the earthquake, the water in the hydrant at that corner gave out after a few minutes, but a good supply was obtained at the corner of Buchanan and Hayes streets."

Naturally, the spreading fire caused even more hysteria among the public. One resident noted, "The fire was going on in the district south of them, and at intervals all night exhausted fire-fighters made their way to the plaza and dropped, with the breath out of them, among the huddled people and the bundles of household goods. The soldiers, who were administering affairs with all the justice of judges and all the devotion of heroes, kept three or four buckets of water, even from the women, for these men, who kept coming all night. There was a little food, also kept by the soldiers for these emergencies, and the sergeant had in his charge one precious bottle of whisky, from which is doled out drinks to those who were utterly exhausted. Over in a corner of the plaza a band of men and women were praying, and one fanatic, driven crazy by horror, was crying out at the top of his voice: 'The Lord sent it, the Lord!' His hysterical crying got on the nerves of the soldiers and bade fair to start a panic among the women and children, so the sergeant went over and stopped it by force. All night they huddled together in this hell, with the fire making it bright as day on all sides; and in the morning the soldiers, using their senses again, commandeered a supply of bread from a bakery, sent out another water squad, and fed the refugees with a semblance of breakfast."

Panoramic views of fires across San Francisco

Incredibly, one witness, a businessman named Jerome Clark, had taken a ferry into San Francisco after the earthquake, so he was on hand to describe the scene near the Bay:

"In every direction from the ferry building flames were seething, and as I stood there, a five-story building half a block away fell with a crash, and the flames swept clear across Market Street and caught a new fireproof building recently erected. The streets in places had sunk three or four feet, in others great humps had appeared four or five feet high. The street car tracks were bent and twisted out of shape. Electric wires lay in every direction. Streets on all sides were filled with brick and mortar, buildings either completely collapsed or brick fronts had just dropped completely off. Wagons with horses hitched to them, drivers and all, lying on the streets, all dead, struck and killed by the falling bricks, these mostly the wagons of the produce dealers, who do the greater part of their work at that hour of the morning. Warehouses and large wholesale houses of all descriptions either down, or walls bulging, or else twisted, buildings moved bodily two or three feet out of line and still standing with walls all cracked.

The Call building, a twelve-story skyscraper, stood and looked all right at first glance, but had moved at the base two feet at one end out into the sidewalk, and the elevators refused to work, all the interior being just twisted out of shape. It afterward burned as I watched it.

Fires were blazing in all directions, and all of the finest and best of the office and business buildings were either burning or surrounded. They pumped water from the bay, but the fire was soon too far away from the water front to make efforts in this direction of much avail. The water mains had been broken by the earthquake, and so there was no supply for the fire engines and they were helpless. The only way out was to dynamite, and I saw some of the finest and most beautiful buildings in the city, new modern palaces, blown to atoms. First they blew up one or two buildings at a time. Finding that of no avail, they took half a block; that was no use; then they took a block; but in spite of them all the fire kept on spreading."

Chapter 5: Water

"We obtained water here about 7 p.m., April 19th, and under the splendid leadership of Chief Murphy, of the 10th Battalion, S.F. Fire Department, we succeeded in checking the fire at this point and saving a block of buildings bounded on the North and West by Montgomery and Jackson Streets. The Appraisers' Building was in the next block to the Eastward, which was also saved at this time. The best work in my opinion, of the crews under my command, was done at this point. The fire chief had the assistance of but two of his own battalion and had no water. This was the only stream of water that ever reached this section of the city; and in feet this was the longest distance that any saltwater stream was taken from the water front -- the distance to the Leslie being a little over eleven blocks." - Lieutenant Frederick Freeman

It was only later, after fighting the first few fires used up their supplies, that the problem became a crisis. Again, Shaughnessy wrote, "The fire which started at Hayes and Gough, several hours after the earthquake, got beyond control by reason of there being no water available within reach, and it swept over the Western Addition east of Octavia and south of Golden Gate Ave.; crossed over Market St. near Ninth, and burned out into the Mission until finally stopped at Twentieth St…"

The firemen soon became very good at finding water, including pumping water from a large puddle caused by a break in the water main on what is now Van Ness Avenue, South. They also pumped water from household wells and commandeered the saltwater held in tanks by the United Railroads at Eleventh and Bryant Streets. One of the most disgusting accounts mentioned that "water was obtained for some time by draughting from the sewers, which were full of water from the broken mains at Seventh and Howard streets."

Of course, there were also a few natural sources of water as well. Shaughnessy mentioned, "The fire which started at Fifth and Minna streets and in the electric light works on Jessie St. near Third, which soon merged into one, were stopped from crossing Market St. by means of two small streams from the north side of Market St., where the pressure, ordinarily above 85 pounds, was about ten pounds."

The buildings nearest the docks were the easiest to save since the firefighters were able to pump an unlimited supply of seawater directly onto the fire, and this was what finally checked the fire damage done to the part of the city known as Chinatown. Home to thousands of hard-working Chinese immigrants who had come to the city to make a living by serving other Chinese arriving daily from around the country, it soon burned to the ground, in spite of the efforts of the firefighters to put out the blaze. The fire department would later be criticized for not fighting the fires in the part of town as hard as they had those in wealthier sections, but Shaughnessy's report details their efforts: "When the fire broke out in the Chinese wash house on Howard St. near Third, Engine Co. 4, whose quarters were across the street, could obtain no water from the hydrant, and was obliged to go to the cistern at Folsom and Second streets, from where a stream was obtained by doubling up with Engine Co. 10. This cistern was soon exhausted, and Engine 35 soon took the cistern at Folsom and First streets, and pumped to other engines, and after this was also exhausted Engine Co. 35 retired to the cistern at First and Harrison streets. The fire had reached such proportions, however, that this cistern, although having a capacity of 100,000 gallons, was drained without checking it, and the companies were forced to go to the foot of Third St., where by draughting from the Bay, the fire was prevented from crossing Townsend St."

Seawater also put out the flames at the end of Howard Street: "At Market and Beale streets, Engine Co. 1 obtained a little water for a short time, but nothing less than a dozen powerful streams could have stopped the fire that was in progress there. The same may be said of the fire that broke out at the same time at Stuart and Market streets, which, however, was checked at Howard St. by streams from the fire boats, assisted by two companies from Oakland."

By this time, both the firemen and their water supplies were becoming increasingly exhausted. Shaughnessy noted, "Engine Co. 1 also obtained water from the hydrant at Davis and California streets, and worked single-handed on a fire adjoining that corner for which, under ordinary conditions, a third alarm would have been sent in. In a short time this fire got beyond control and went to Market St. and the company was obliged to retire."

The story began to repeat itself over and over again; on Clay and Davis Streets, "no water was obtainable," so the firemen "retired to the cisterns at DuPont…All these cisterns were exhausted, while the fire was still advancing…" At Powell and California and Sacramento and Clay, Shaughnessy reported, "After a while these hydrants ran dry and the companies were forced to retire. Then the cistern at California and Mason streets was made use of in a desperate but unsuccessful effort to save the Hopkins Art Institute."

As they worked, the men became both more desperate and more discouraged. They lost City Hall to the "Hayes Valley Fire" but finally stopped it at Eddy Street. There were still working hydrants near the corner of Eddy and Van Ness, but the ones at Franklin Street were dry. When the fire at the Knickerbocker Hotel jumped the street and its sparks set fire to a building at the corner of California and Van Ness, Shaughnessy explained, "It was found that the nearest hydrant from which water could be obtained was at Bush and Laguna streets, and in order to reach the fire on California St., four engines had to be put in line. By the time this was done, the fire had crossed Sacramento and California streets and was burning up to Franklin St. in three blocks; when it was almost checked there, fire suddenly broke out in Kelly's stable on the south side of Pine St. near Franklin, and on account of the large frame buildings on the west side of Franklin St. there was great danger that the fire would cross that street and get beyond control."

Some of the most notorious incidents of the disaster truly put into perspective how helpless the city's officials felt when trying to battle the fires. A city resident named Adolphus Busch remembered, "The most terrible thing I saw was the futile struggle of a policeman and others to rescue a man who was pinned down in burning wreckage. The helpless man watched it in silence till the fire began burning his feet. Then he screamed and begged to be killed. The policeman took his name and address and shot him through the head." Max Fast recounted a similar tale: "When the fire caught the Windsor Hotel at Fifth and Market Streets there were three men on the roof, and it was impossible to get them down. Rather than see the crazed men fall in with the roof and be roasted alive the military officer directed his men to shoot them, which they did in the presence of 5,000 people."

Chapter 6: Dynamite

"By Wednesday afternoon, inside of twelve hours, half the heart of the city was gone. At that time I watched the vast conflagration from out on the bay. It was dead calm. Not a flicker of wind stirred. Yet from every side wind was pouring in upon the city. East, west, north, and south, strong winds were blowing upon the doomed city. The heated air rising made an enormous suck. Thus did the fire of itself build its own colossal chimney through the atmosphere. Day and night this dead calm continued, and yet, near to the flames, the wind was often half a gale, so mighty was the suck. Wednesday night saw the destruction of the very heart of the city. Dynamite was lavishly used, and many of San Francisco proudest structures were crumbled by man himself into ruins, but there was no withstanding the onrush of the flames. Time and again successful stands were made by the fire-fighters, and every time the flames flanked around on either side or came up from the rear, and turned to defeat the hard-won victory." - Jack London

It took three more engines to finally stop the spread of the fire at Sutter Street, but according to Shaughnessy, "Meanwhile the fire was spreading north unchecked on the east side of Van Ness Ave. until it reached Vallejo St., where Engine Co. 3, securing water from the hydrant at Green and Gough streets, and pumping to Engine Co. 20, fought the fire back to Polk St., only to lose its water at a critical time and be forced to move to Union and Gough." Finally, with the help of a fire boat supplied by the federal government, the fire was stopped at the corner of Union and Van Ness Avenue, but that was just one fire. Many others burned on, and even in recollection, Shaughnessy's report became more frantic: "In the meantime the fire was spreading over Russian Hill, and descending on the North Beach district. As there was not a drop of water in any of the mains, the companies were forced to resort to the remaining cisterns in that district, most of which had a capacity of only 20,000 gallons and were rapidly exhausted without materially checking the fire…A stream was also led from a Government boat at Filbert St. pier to Broadway and Powell streets, but without avail. The fire was then sweeping over Telegraph Hill rendering it impossible to reach the only unused cistern at DuPont and Greenwich streets, and the companies were forced to retire to the Seawall in a final effort to stay the conflagration. Streams were led up Stockton, Powell and Mason streets but the men were steadily driven back, until the fire worked around them to the west, and, driven by a strong west wind which had sprung up, swept down on the Seawall and forced them to beat a hasty retreat to Lombard St., where the fire on the water front was stopped with a stream from a boat, and the Merchants' Cold Storage plant was saved by the same means."

As the main water supplies were running out, the army came up with a new and radical solution for stopping the fire: using dynamite to destroy buildings standing in the fire's path. The idea was that these fallen buildings would create a sort of fire break that would spare the structures behind them. It was a radical and very controversial solution, but as the 18th wore on and the fires still burned, no one had any better ideas. Thus, the red batons of destruction were carefully transported from the California Powder Company at Pinole and carried to men who were expert in using them. Throughout the night, blast after blast lit up the sky, accompanied so often by shaking ground that people seemed to stop noticing it and little children slept soundly on.

In the years that followed, the army would be blamed for much of the destruction of the city. Many would say that the officers in charged had destroyed buildings unnecessarily and that all would have been well without their work. Others would point out that the use of the dynamite didn't really stop any of the fires and that they burned on anyway. However, those people had the benefit of hindsight and analysis, and it's not entirely fair to criticize people who were dealing with the disaster at the time and were ready to try anything.

Many would record their impressions of San Francisco bathed in the light of a thousand burning fires, but few did it as well as the famous author Jack London, who wrote, "Before the flames, throughout the night, fled tens of thousands of homeless ones. Some were wrapped in blankets. Others carried bundles of bedding and dear household treasures. Sometimes a whole family was harnessed to a carriage or delivery wagon that was weighted down with their possessions. Baby buggies, toy wagons, and go-carts were used as trucks, while every other person was dragging a trunk. Yet everybody was gracious. The most perfect courtesy obtained. Never in all San Francisco's history, were her people so kind and courteous as on this night of terror…All night these tens of thousands fled before the flames. Many of them, the poor people from the labor ghetto, had fled all day as well. They had left their homes burdened with possessions. Now and again they lightened up, flinging out upon the street clothing and treasures they had dragged for miles."

Ultimately, the dynamite didn't do much good and the fires raged on until they burned themselves out four days after the earthquake. By that time, thousands of people had died and millions of dollars in property had been lost. In fact, one historian estimates that the value of the property lost in the city was approximately equivalent to the budget of the entire federal government that year. What is known is that the earthquake and fires combined to destroy nearly 500 city blocks and 25,000 buildings, leaving over a quarter of a million people homeless.

A picture of Market St. laying in ruins

Picture of the ruins of Fourth St. just off Market St.

Chapter 7: Martial Law

A depiction of Army soldiers providing goods to San Francisco

Soldiers standing among the ruins

HALL OF JUSTICE

Soldiers pose outside the Hall of Justice

"Throughout this whole day constant trouble had been experienced owing to the large number of drunken people along the waterfront. My force was unarmed with the exception of the officers, who carried revolvers; and the police, of whom I only saw two, were absolutely helpless. The crowds rushed saloon after saloon and looted the stocks becoming intoxicated early in the day. In my opinion great loss of life resulted from men and women becoming stupefied by liquor and being too tired and exhausted to get out of the way of the fire. During this whole day we needed unarmed men to rescue women and children in the neighborhood of Rincon Hill, the fire having made a clean sweep of this poor residence district in about an hour's time. The most heartrending sights were witnessed in this neighborhood, but with my handful of men we could not do as much for the helpless as we wished. Able-bodied men refused to work with the fire department, stating that they would not work for less than forty cents an hour, etc. Men refused to aid old and crippled men and women out of the way of the fire and only thought of themselves." - Lieutenant Frederick Freeman

Society likes to believe that a disaster brings out the best in people, and it often does. Arnold Genthe, who had been at the opera house the night before, told of his breakfast the morning of the disaster: "Inside the hotel…there was no gas or electricity, but somehow hot coffee was available which, with bread and butter and fruit, made a satisfying breakfast. When I asked the waiter for a check he announced with a wave of his hand, 'No charge today, sir. Everyone is welcome as long as things hold out.'"

At the same time, panic and terror also bring out the worst in people, and that was why, while many of the soldiers and sailors dispatched to San Francisco kept busy working to put out fires and dig out those who were trapped, others had their hands full trying to keep order. There were a number of problems keeping law enforcement officers busy. The first and most pressing issue was trying to rescue those who were trapped, but while there were also a few good Samaritans who pitched in to help look for survivors, most people were too concerned about their own safety and that of their families to take an active interest in others. Others insisted that they would only work if paid for their labor, and paid well at that.

The second issue was the swelling masses of people taking to the streets and trying to get out of town. Bailey Millard described one scene: "Automobiles piled high with bedding and hastily snatched stores, tooted wild warnings amid the crowds. Drays loaded with furniture and swarming over with men, women and children, struggled over the earthquake-torn street, their horses sometimes falling by the wayside in a vain effort to pass some bad fissure in the 'made' ground. Cabs, for which fares at the rate of ten to twenty dollars apiece had been paid in advance, dotted the procession, and there were vans, express wagons of all sorts, buggies and carts, all loaded down with passengers and goods."

On April 20, the USS *Chicago* rescued more than 20,000 people who had run toward the harbor while trying to escape the spreading fire. The ships spent the entire day sailing back and forth across San Francisco Bay, ferrying as many people as it could safely carry across to safer shores. It remains the largest evacuation of a civilian population by sea in history and rivals the more famous evacuation of Dunkirk that took place during World War II.

The third problem was how to feed and care for the large number of people who did not make it out of the city. The crisis of food and shelter fell on the wealthy and the poor alike, as it did not matter how much food one might have had at home once the homes were gone. Funston sent out a request for food and tents to all nearby military establishments, and the following morning, he received word from the Secretary of State, William Howard Taft, that all the tents the United States Army had to spare were on their way to San Francisco.

Ernest Adams, a respected citizen, observed "The city is under martial law and we are living on the government, or at least many are. As soon as the good were safe, I cleaned out the nearest grocery store of canned goods and we are living in tents, cooking meals on a few bricks piled up Dutch-oven style." Another man, David Hill, described the lives of the newly homeless: "When daylight came we helped cook our breakfast in the street where rich and poor alike squat side by side cooking on brick stoves, and then all go stand in line to get their share of provisions. No one is allowed to sell a thing there but everything left in stores has been distributed, and loads are coming in every day."

Picture of a camp that housed refugees

Picture of refugees in front of a tent

The fourth and most dangerous issue surrounded how to protect private property. At 3:00 on the afternoon of the 18th, Mayor Schmitz met with the city leader to appoint a "Committee of Fifty" made up of men he trusted to lead San Francisco in a time of crisis. During the meeting, he stated emphatically, "Let it be given out that three men have already been shot down without mercy for looting. Let it also be understood that the order has been given to all soldiers and policemen to do likewise without hesitation in the cases of any and all miscreants who may seek to take advantage of the city's awful misfortune." As good as his word, he followed up that statement with handbills that were tacked up all over town. They read:

> "The Federal Troops, the members of the Regular Police Force and all Special Police Officers have been authorized by me to KILL any and all persons found engaging in Looting or in the Commission of Any Other Crime.
>
> I have directed all the Gas and Electric Lighting Co.'s not to turn on Gas or Electricity until I order them to do so. You may therefore expect the city to remain in darkness for an indefinite time.

I request all citizens to remain at home from darkness until daylight every night until order is restored.

I WARN all Citizens of the danger of fire from Damaged or Destroyed Chimneys, Broken or Leaking Gas Pipes or Fixtures, or any like cause."

While his order seems extreme, it was not challenged by anyone in authority when it was put into place. In fact, some might say that it was too strictly enforced. David Hill later recalled of that first night: "At 5 o'clock a rifle shot was heard on the block and some young fellow fell dead who was imprudent enough to venture out to borrow some whiskey for his sick mother. A soldier ordered him to throw it away and shot him for refusing. This is only one of many cases."

A picture of soldiers looting pairs of shoes in the middle of Market St.

Chapter 8: Burning Bigotry

"One of the evils springing from the late disaster to San Francisco…is the great influx of Chinese into this city from San Francisco. Not only have they pushed outward the limits of Oakland's heretofore constricted and insignificant Chinatown, but they have settled themselves in large colonies throughout the residence parts of the city, bringing with them their vices and their filth. The residence of C.H. King...has been leased to Chinese, and now the house is crowded with Mongolians, 60 or 70 occupying the premises. Already this house...has taken on the air of a Chinese hangout. It is a rendezvous for scores of Celestials, who shuffle in and out of the place, for what purpose, one familiar with their life can easily conjecture. The residents of the neighborhood, many of them members of Oakland's most exclusive society, are up in arms, and will appeal to the authorities to abate this nuisance." - *The Oakland Herald*, April 27, 1906

Once the fires were out and the city began to think of rebuilding, the underlying issue of racism surfaced. For decades, San Francisco had been the home of a large number of Chinese immigrants, and in keeping with the standards of the time, they mostly lived in Chinatown. However, the fire destroyed that section of town and left most of its citizens just as homeless as the wealthiest white politicians. At first, there were rumors that the Asian-Americans were not receiving the same number and quality of rations as were their white neighbors, an issue so scandalous that it was reported in the newspapers back east and led to a directive straight from the White House that everyone be cared for equally.

However, by the time the directive made its way through to San Francisco, most of the people in question had left town and headed to nearby Oakland, where they were able to use their culture's famous familial ties to find places to live. As the shocking quote above demonstrates, Oakland's own bigotry cried out against this influx of immigrants, but San Francisco soon cried out against it as well, albeit for different reasons. According to an article in the *San Francisco Chronicle* on May 2, 1906, entitled *Now Fear That The Chinese May Abandon City*, "Charles S. Wheeler informed the committee [on Chinese affairs] that he had been in consultation with the first secretary of the Chinese legation on the preceding day, and cautioned the committee, before taking any action, to look well into the future and inform itself thoroughly as to what influence its action might have on the future of San Francisco. He declared that if the situation were not wisely handled the bulk of San Francisco's Oriental trade might be diverted to other Pacific Coast ports. Seattle was making a strong bid for this trade, he declared, and would like to welcome the Chinese of this city. By the exercise of caution and diplomacy, he thought San Francisco might still retain its large Oriental trade, and at the same time look after its own civic affairs."

As always, it was that last bit about "look after its own civic affairs" that presented the problem. San Francisco saw its "civic affairs" as primarily serving the needs of it wealthy white population. The city leaders also knew that the section of the city that had previously housed Chinatown was prime real estate that others had wanted to get their hands on for years. Thus, they were anxious to try to pick a new, less attractive section of the city to offer to Chinese residents when they returned. This would prove to be a problem that would get the attention of everyone from the mayor to the President of the United States and even the royal family of China. Fortunately, a satisfactory arrangement was found, and the Asian-Americans returned to

San Francisco to eventually become a valued part of society.

Moreover, there were those in the community who were not just willing to help the Chinese in their city but had been doing so for years. The Occidental Board Mission Home for Chinese Girls was run by the famous missionary Donaldina Cameron. She remained as devoted to her charges, many of whom had been rescued from slavery, on that day as she had all the other days she had been in charge of the home. Though their building survived, they were soon forced to evacuate the premises because of approaching fire. Cameron later wrote, "To have our Chinese girls on the streets among these crowds after nightfall was a danger too great to risk. As hastily, therefore, as we could work amidst the confusion and excitement, we gathered some bedding, a little food, and a few garments together and the last of the girls left the Mission Home. They tramped the long distance to Van Ness Avenue carrying what they could. On the way the children joined the party, and the entire family was at last established for the night in the Presbyterian Church ... the small children and babies were carefully cared for through all the excitement. There were three babies— the tiny Ah Ping, not a month old, had to be tenderly carried by the girls; her poor little mother (a rescued slave) was too feeble and helpless to aid much. Hatsu had her wee baby, only three months old, and little Ah Chung, eighteen months, was equally helpless..."

Donaldina Cameron

The next morning, they made one last trip to the mission house, which the fire had not yet reached, and got what provisions they could carry out. From there, they set out on the long journey, on foot, to the ferry, where they successfully pleaded for passage across to the Seminary at San Anselmo. She later described their will to go on by writing, "As tears would not avail…laughter was the tonic which stimulated that weary, unwashed, and uncombed procession on the long tramp through stifling, crowded streets near where the fire raged, and through the desolate district already burned, where fires of yesterday still smoldered."

Chapter 9: Rising from the Ashes

Panoramic views of San Francisco in ruins

Aerial view of San Francisco's remains

"The earthquake period is gone. Once the pent up forces of nature have had a vent, nothing of a serious nature need be apprehended. At the most a succession of minor shocks may be felt and that's all. It is not unreasonable, therefore, for people to continue in dread of a new destructive temblor. People should fearlessly go to work and repair mischief done and sleep quietly at night anywhere at all, especially in wooden frame. Never mind foreboders of evil: they do not know what they are talking about. Seismonetry is in its infancy and those therefore who venture out with predictions of future earthquakes when the main shock has taken place ought to be arrested as disturbers of the peace." - Father Ricard, April 22, 1906

Even in the midst of the disaster, many businessmen were as worried about their inventories as they were their lives. Within a week of the disaster, Ernest Adams had contacted his superiors at the famous Reed and Barton silver company and given them a full report of all he did to save their inventory: "Reaching the office, I waded through plaster, etc., to find the goods still in the cases but off the shelves without any damage being done them. Locking the doors again I rushed to street…I gathered up a force of seven men, stationed them at our office doors, and started for a truck…Fortunately I had two guns in the office, and stationing one man at the entrance and one on the truck with orders to shoot, the balance of us went to work, and that dray man pulled the heaviest load of his life. I saved all of the Sterling Hollow and Flat Ware with the exception of a few Flat Ware samples in the trays beside my books, stock sterling and plated ware books. The plated ware, it was impossible to touch, as the flames were then upon us…."

Adams went on to devote himself to protecting his prized inventory, hauling it from place to place and keeping it in his personal possession until he was able to once more secure it in a shop: "All Wednesday night we guarded the treasure, but the fire kept creeping toward us, driving the people back to the Cliff House, the western extremity of the Peninsula, and Thursday I was again forced to move the goods westward. The last stand was our back yard, two miles from the first stand, and I am now with our sterling goods, the remains of our beautiful office. The city is under martial law and we are living on the government, or at least many are…With this valuable property under my care I could not afford to take any chances, and I have stayed close to my cache."

Mr. Bacigalupi had even more concern for his business, since his inventory of phonograph records and musical instruments was a huge investment on his part: "I ran down to my store, trying to unfasten the door, but the lock was so hot [from the approaching fire] that in trying to unfasten same I scorched my fingers. I worked for what seemed to be an hour, but which in reality must have been from twenty to thirty seconds." After finally getting inside, he was surprised and grieved by what he saw: "You can imagine my feelings on going to the second floor where my Phonograph salesroom was located, and seeing every Record standing on its shelf in perfect order, just as though there had been no earthquake at all…to think that the Pianos had been thrown down on their faces, and Records, which stood by the thousands on our shelves, had not been moved."

In spite of the loss of his five story building and a lot its contents, Bacigalupi was able to recognize the opportunity that the disaster was offering him. He wrote to a friend that "while the fire was still burning close to the store from which I am now writing, I secured this good location at a nominal cost for my Phonograph business. One week later I was offered three times what I am paying for rent, but I refused. I am now engaged in the real estate business; have opened a market place two blocks from the main street of New 'Frisco, and am also interested in a restaurant, cigar stand, and last and most important of all—the Phonograph business…I have decided to use this store, which is centrally located, in which to retail talking machines of all the leading makes, and am putting up my own building on leased ground, two blocks from here, in which to conduct the business of jobbing Edison Phonographs, which has been my chief occupation for the last eight years." Understanding that those to whom he was writing might be surprised by his decision to start again from scratch at 51 years old, he added, "I am game, and intend to go to it now as I did then. I have taken into the firm my two sons, with the aid of whom I believe I will be able to do a better and larger business in talking machines than has ever been done in the West…Regardless of all those ordeals I AM GOING TO STICK WITH 'FRISCO."

Many others would join him in "sticking with 'Frisco." Surprisingly to some, most of the people that had lived in the community before the disaster moved back into their homes as soon as they were given the all clear. Their reasons for staying were as varied as their individual backgrounds, but many had no choice because they were too poor to be able to afford to move anywhere else. Others, like Bacigalupi, saw an opportunity to make a profit from rebuilding.

People like Bacigalupi turned out to be mostly right, because the city did rise from the ashes at an incredible rate. Within a decade, San Francisco was bigger and more prosperous than it had ever been before. Arnold Genthe was a witness to that rebirth: "Among the many telegrams I received was one from Edward Sothern and Julia Marlowe. 'Now that you have lost everything,' it read, 'you should come to New York. We will see that you find a fully equipped studio waiting for you, so that you can start work without delay.' It was heartening and consoling to have this fine proof of real friendship. The temptation was great, but I was not willing to leave San Francisco then. I wanted to stay, to see the new city which would rise out of the ruins. I felt that my place was there. I had something to contribute, even if only in a small measure, to the rebuilding of the city. I started my search for a new studio. It would take years before the business section would be rebuilt. No one knew exactly just where the new center of the city was to be. Location was unimportant. On Clay Street, not far from the gates of the Presidio I discovered a picturesque one-story cottage. In its small garden was a fine old scrub-oak, and I believe it was this and not so much the house that made me decide to take a five-year lease. My friends encouraged me. 'Don't worry about being so far out. We'll come anyway, no matter where you are. The chief thing is for you to have a place that you like and where…you can work.' And so I started to make a few structural changes and to get together the necessary equipment that would enable me to continue my work as a portrait photographer."

Some people saw the earthquake as source of spiritual inspiration. Just like those who fell to their knees in prayer as the city shook down around them, so they continued to look to strength from a higher power throughout their experience. To them, the earthquake was yet another opportunity to find truth and beauty in a fallen world. One such woman was Emma Burke, who later wrote that "this stupendous disaster leads a thoughtful person to two conclusions: viz., faith in humanity; and the progress of the human race. All artificial restraints of our civilization fell away with the earthquake's shocks. Every man was his brother's keeper. Everyone spoke to everyone else with a smile. The all-prevailing cheerfulness and helpfulness were encouraging signs of our progress in practicing the golden rule, and humanity's struggle upward toward the example of our Savior."

Of course, the reason most people stayed was as simple as it was meaningful: San Francisco was home. Many of them had come west as young men searching for gold. Some of them had found it, and many stayed to help build up the city. The 49ers were now old men and disinclined to start over anywhere else. Others had come to the city from the other side of the world and had worked hard for years to raise enough money to bring their families to join them. They dreamed of a time when they could leave their small businesses to their sons and grandsons. Many had been born in the city and knew no other place to live. They were just as determined to rebuild the city itself as they were their own homes.

Howard Livingston, speaking decades later, described his family's life in the aftermath of the disaster, and how their belief in their city's ultimate destiny drove them back into the town rather than away from it: "A few days after the fire ended, my mother and the younger children returned to our home, and I found work at the warehouse of a wholesale drug company which opened in a temporary location. Everyone was busy, and I frequently heard people say that the new San Francisco would be a far finer city than the one which had been destroyed. Some weeks later the Vulcan Iron Works reopened, and I found employment in their structural steel department. I worked on the steel framing of some of the first new buildings erected after the fire. Five generations of my family have lived in San Francisco. It is a city for which I feel great affection, and I have always been glad that I was able to have a small part in its rebuilding."

Bibliography

Aitken, Frank W.; Edward Hilton (1906). A History Of The Earthquake And Fire In San Francisco. San Francisco: The Edward Hilton Co.

Banks, Charles Eugene; Opie Percival Read (1906). The History Of The San Francisco Disaster And Mount Vesuvius Horror. C. E. Thomas.

Bronson, William (1959). *The Earth Shook, the Sky Burned*. Doubleday.

Double Cone Quarterly, Fall Equinox, volume VII, Number 3 (2004).

Greely, Adolphus W. (1906). Earthquake In California, April 18, 1906. Special Report On The Relief Operations Conducted By The Military Authorities. Washington: Government Printing Office.

Jordan, David Starr; John Casper Branner, Charles Derleth, Jr., Stephen Taber, F. Omari, Harold W. Fairbanks, Mary Hunter Austin (1907). *The California Earthquake of 1906*. San Francisco: A. M. Robertson.

Keeler, Charles (1906). San Francisco Through Earthquake And Fire. San Francisco: Paul Elder And Company.

London, Jack. "The Story of an Eyewitness". London's report from the scene. Originally published in Collier's Magazine. May 5, 1906.

Morris, Charles (1906). The San Francisco Calamity By Earthquake And Fire

Schussler, Hermann (1907). The Water Supply Of San Francisco, California Before, During And After The Earthquake of April 18, 1906 And The Subsequent Conflagration. New York: Martin B. Brown Press.

Tyler, Sydney; Harry Fielding Reid (1908, 1910). *The California Earthquake of April 18, 1906: Report of The State Earthquake Investigation Commission, Volumes I and II*. Washington, D.C.: The Carnegie Institution of Washington.

Tyler, Sydney; Ralph Stockman Tarr (1908). San Francisco's Great Disaster. Philadelphia: P. W. Ziegler Co.

Wald, David J.; Kanamori, Hiroo; Helmberger, Donald V.; Heaton, Thomas H. (1993), "Source study of the 1906 San Francisco Earthquake", *Bulletin of the Seismological Society of America* (Seismological Society of America) **83** (4): 981–1019

Winchester, Simon, *A Crack in the Edge of the World: America and the Great California Earthquake of 1906*. HarperCollins Publishers, New York, 2005.

Made in the USA
Monee, IL
30 January 2022

90244988R00030